NOISE FROM HEART

NEHABIJU

Copyright © Nehabiju
All Rights Reserved.

This book has been published with all efforts taken to make the material error-free after the consent of the author. However, the author and the publisher do not assume and hereby disclaim any liability to any party for any loss, damage, or disruption caused by errors or omissions, whether such errors or omissions result from negligence, accident, or any other cause.

While every effort has been made to avoid any mistake or omission, this publication is being sold on the condition and understanding that neither the author nor the publishers or printers would be liable in any manner to any person by reason of any mistake or omission in this publication or for any action taken or omitted to be taken or advice rendered or accepted on the basis of this work. For any defect in printing or binding the publishers will be liable only to replace the defective copy by another copy of this work then available.

Contents

DHARD

Chapter1

Mere dhard mein ek sukoon hai

Mere dhard ek intezaar hai

Mere dhard mein ansoon hai

Mere dhard mein ek kamosi hai

Mere dhard mein ek raaz hai

Mere dhard mein tum hoon

Tere dosti

Chapter2

Tere liye

Chapter3

Har rang mein mil jaun tere liye

Har asun mein doob jaun tere liye

Har kamosshi mein chup jaun tere liye

Har kushi mein sawar jaun tere liye.

Tum

Chapter4

Tum mere nahi yeh jaan chuki hoon mein
Tumhari chahare ko bool chuki hoon mein
Tum aa na aaye hum na aaye
Tum hamare nahi yeh jaan chuki hoom mein

badlaav

Chapter5

Ghadi ki samay badalti hai,
Jaisehi insanka dil badalta hai.
Jaise sangeet main swaar badalti hai,
Jaise he insan mein pyar badalte hai.
Jaise har mahine mosam badlte hai,
Vesehi hamare dost bhi badalte hai.

Sirf meri ho

Chapter6

• 23 •

Jab sab ke nazre tere ore ho

Mere nazrom me tum

Jab sab ki lavzom me tum ho

Mere muskan ho tum

Jab sab ki anken tum hye he dheke

Tere ankoka kajal ko tade

Yeh dhil ko patta hai ki

Tum sirf meri ho

Sirf meri .

pyar kar na galat nahi hai, lekin use pyar mein ko jaana galat hai